# CLIMATE CHANGE

NANCY DICKMANN

Published by Brown Bear Books Ltd
4877 N. Circulo Bujia
Tucson, AZ 85718
USA

and

Studio G14, Regent Studios,
1 Thane Villas, London N7 7PH, UK

© 2023 Brown Bear Books Ltd

ISBN 978-1-78121-814-3 (library bound)
ISBN 978-1-78121-820-4 (paperback)

All rights reserved. No part of this book may be reproduced, stored in a retrieval system or transmitted in any form or by any means, electronic, mechanical, photocopying, recording or otherwise, without the prior written permission of the copyright holder.

Library of Congress Cataloging-in-Publication Data available on request

Design: squareandcircus.co.uk
Design Manager: Keith Davis
Children's Publisher: Anne O'Daly

Manufactured in the United States of America
CPSIA compliance information: Batch#AG/5652

**Picture Credits**
The photographs in this book are used by permission and through the courtesy of:

iStock: branex 8–9, Imgorthand 20–21, mg studio 6–7; Shutterstock: Alones 4–5, Jesus Cobleda 18–19, maloff 12–13, Toa55 14–15, Ulga 10–11, Vlad61 16–17.

All other artwork and photography © Brown Bear Books.

t-top, r-right, l-left, c-center, b-bottom

Brown Bear Books has made every attempt to contact the copyright holder. If you have any information about omissions, please contact: licensing@brownbearbooks.co.uk

**Websites**
The website addresses in this book were valid at the time of going to press. However, it is possible that contents or addresses may change following publication of this book.
No responsibility for any such changes can be accepted by the author or the publisher. Readers should be supervised when they access the Internet.

Words in **bold** appear in the Glossary on page 23.

# CONTENTS

Weather and Climate.....................4
The Greenhouse Effect ................6
Greenhouse Gases .......................8
Fossil Fuels...................................10
Changing Oceans .........................12
Extreme Weather .......................14
Animals and Climate Change........16
Stopping Climate Change .............18
What Can We Do?........................20
Quiz ...............................................22
Glossary .......................................23
Find out More ..............................24
Index..............................................24

# WEATHER AND CLIMATE

Is it rainy or sunny outside today? Is it cold or warm? Whatever the answer, this is the weather. Wind and snow are kinds of weather. So are storms and **heat waves**. The weather changes from day to day.

## WHAT IS CLIMATE?

**Climate** is not quite the same as weather. It is the average weather over a long time. Do you live in a place with cold winters? This is part of the climate. One winter day may be sunny. The next might be snowy. But they are part of a long-term pattern of cold weather.

Earth is surrounded by a blanket of gases. It's called the **atmosphere**. This is where weather happens.

# Climate Zones

Different areas have different climates. Here are some of the main ones.

A tropical area is hot all year round. There is plenty of rain.

A temperate area has warm summers and mild winters. There are thunderstorms in the summers.

Summers in continental areas are a bit cooler. Winters are very cold. There are often blizzards.

A dry area has very little rain. Some dry areas are hot. Others are cold.

Polar areas are very cold and icy all year round.

# THE GREENHOUSE EFFECT

We get light and heat from the Sun. Without it, life couldn't exist. Too close to the Sun, and Earth would be too hot. Too far away, and it would be too cold. Scientists call our location the "Goldilocks zone." That's because it is just right!

## CARBON DIOXIDE

Earth is getting warmer. But we are not getting closer to the Sun. There is a gas called **carbon dioxide** ($CO_2$) in the atmosphere. Humans breathe it out. Burning **fuels** like gas releases it. There is now more $CO_2$ than ever before. It causes the **greenhouse effect**.

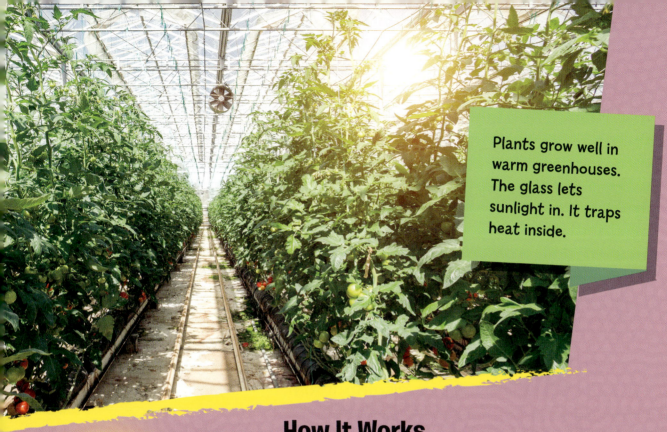

Plants grow well in warm greenhouses. The glass lets sunlight in. It traps heat inside.

## How It Works

There are many gases in our atmosphere. Some act like the glass in a greenhouse.

**1.** The Sun sends out **energy**.

**2.** Some energy bounces off the atmosphere. It goes back into space.

**3.** Some energy goes through. It reaches the ground.

**4.** The energy warms up the land and oceans. They release heat.

**5.** Some of the heat escapes into space.

**6.** Some heat gets trapped by the greenhouse gases. It stays in the atmosphere. This warms the planet's climate.

# GREENHOUSE GASES

**Tracking Methane**
Methane is invisible. But new **satellites** can spot leaks. They fly high above the Earth. Once they report a leak, it can be fixed.

Different gases cause the greenhouse effect. They are called greenhouses gases. They trap heat and warm the planet. Water vapor is one. It is water in gas form. It forms when water **evaporates** from oceans.

## METHANE

Methane is another greenhouse gas. Do you use natural gas for cooking or heating? Methane is part of it. Some methane forms naturally. Swamps release it. It comes from dead plants and animals being broken down.

## Where Methane Comes From

More than half the methane in the atmosphere is our fault. Here is where it comes from.

Cows and other farm animals release methane.

We bury trash underground. It slowly breaks down. This releases methane.

We use coal, oil, and natural gas. Methane escapes when we drill for these fuels. It also escapes when we store and ship them.

Cows produce methane in their stomachs. It comes out as burps or farts.

# FOSSIL FUELS

**Locked Away**
Fossil fuels formed millions of years ago. The carbon in them was locked away. It gets released when we burn them. This raises $CO_2$ levels.

We release more $CO_2$ than any other greenhouse gas. Most of it comes from burning **fossil fuels**. Coal, oil, and natural gas are fossil fuels. They come from deep underground. We use them every day. They are our main source of energy.

## ELECTRICITY

A lot of $CO_2$ comes from power plants. These are factories that make **electricity**. Many power plants burn coal. Others burn oil or natural gas. There is energy in the fuels. Power plants turn it into electricity.

## Using Fossil Fuels

Coal, oil, and gas have many uses.

Burned in power plants.

Used for making steel.

An ingredient for making plastic.

Turned into fuels for cars, trains, and planes.

**Coal**

**Oil**

Used for heating.

Burned in power plants.

Used for heating and cooking.

**Gas**

An ingredient for making fertilizer.

Fossil fuels have carbon in them. When they burn, carbon joins with oxygen in the air. This makes $CO_2$.

# CHANGING OCEANS

The greenhouse effect is warming the planet. This causes climate change. We are already seeing its effects. Tides make the ocean rise and fall each day. But scientists can measure the average level. Sea levels are rising around the world. This causes flooding in coastal areas.

## MELTING ICE

Some of Earth's water is frozen. It forms ice caps at the poles. In the Arctic, they float on the water. But climate change is melting the ice caps. The melted water goes into the ocean. This makes sea levels rise.

Seawater expands when it warms up. This makes sea levels rise even more.

## Arctic Ice

Ice in the Arctic changes every year. But we can still see patterns.

There is more ice in winter. It covers a huge area of sea and land.

In summer, some of the ice melts. It will freeze again in winter. This map shows the ice in summer 1979.

In summer 2021, the ice was much smaller.

# EXTREME WEATHER

There is more to climate change than just feeling warmer. Earth's weather is a delicate balance. Even a small rise in temperature can have big effects. We are already seeing more extreme weather. This is because of climate change.

## HEATING UP

Climate change is causing heat waves. They can last for days. The air is very hot. Heat waves can lead to droughts. A drought is a long time with little rain. There is not enough rain to grow crops.

Heat waves dry out trees and plants. This makes them burn easily. Fires can spread quickly.

### Where's the Water?

Climate change causes droughts. It also causes heavy rain. This may seem strange. But the water lost in a drought doesn't disappear. It just falls as rain somewhere else.

## The New Water Cycle

Water moves from the oceans to the sky and back down again. This is the water cycle. Climate change makes it more extreme.

1. There is more heat from the Sun.

2. More water evaporates from the oceans.

3. There is more water in the air. It forms clouds.

4. Rain is heavier than usual.

5. A lot of rain falls in a short time. This causes floods.

# Animals and Climate Change

The corals in a coral reef are animals. If the water is too warm, they turn white. This is not healthy.

Animals are also affected by climate change. When the climate changes, so do their **habitats**. Plants that lived in one area may not be able to survive there any more. That means less food for animals. If they can't find new food sources, they might die.

## SHARING THE LAND

Humans and animals share the land. We all need water and food. Climate change is making these harder to find. Animals must go further to find what they need. They are forced closer to towns. Bears might dig through trash. Lions might kill farm animals.

## Adapt or Die

Here is how climate change is affecting some animals.

Polar bears walk on sea ice to find food. Less ice means it's harder to hunt. Polar bears may die out.

The gang-gang cockatoo's habitat is getting hotter. These birds are growing bigger beaks. This helps them cool down.

Australia saw huge fires in 2019 and 2020. Many koalas died. Others lost their homes.

Whales must go closer to shore to find food. But humans fish near shore. The whales get tangled in fishing nets.

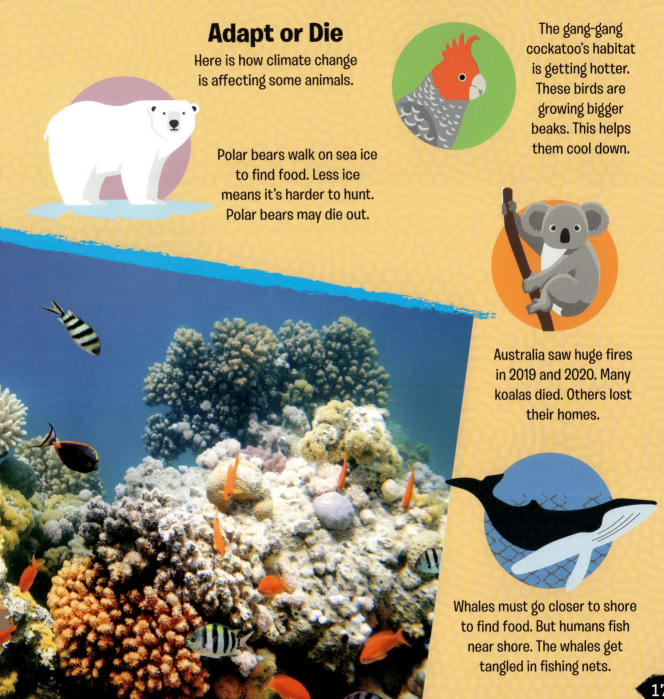

# STOPPING CLIMATE CHANGE

Climate change is already happening. Earth's average temperature is rising. But it's not too late! We need to give out less $CO_2$. If we do, it will slow the pace of climate change. It might even reverse it.

## SCIENCE TO THE RESCUE!

Scientists are working on new ideas to help. We might be able to capture $CO_2$ from the air. Then it would be stored safely. We can use drones to plant trees. We might even put chemicals into the air. These chemicals would block sunlight.

This seaweed can be added to cattle food. Cows that eat it produce less methane.

## Making Changes

Stopping climate change means big changes in the way we live. Here are some of the most important changes.

**No more fossil fuels.** Leave them in the ground!

**New sources of energy.** More wind, solar, and water power.

**Protect our forests.** Trees keep $CO_2$ out of the atmosphere.

**Reduce plastic use.** Making plastic releases $CO_2$.

**Better ways to travel.** Electric cars, buses, and trains.

# WHAT CAN WE DO?

Climate change is a big problem. It might seem too big to solve. But you can make a difference. Even little things can help! You can't build a wind farm. But you can still make climate-friendly changes.

## USING LESS

Making things uses energy. Sending them to stores uses energy, too. Clothes, gadgets, toys, and books all come with a $CO_2$ price. Reducing what we use means less $CO_2$. Only buy what you really need. Try to reuse or recycle whatever you can.

## Climate-Friendly Eating
What we eat has a big impact.

**Make Your Voice Heard**
Our elected officials have a duty to listen. Tell them how you feel about climate change. What new laws would you like to see? You can write a letter or use social media.

**Eat Less Meat**
Raising animals produces a lot of greenhouse gases.

**Switch Your Milk**
Soy, oat, and nut milks are better for the planet.

**Stick to Plants**
They're good for you, and good for the planet.

Think about each car journey. Could you walk or bike instead? Could you take the bus?

**Buy Local Foods in Season**
Foods grown nearby don't need to be shipped as far.

**Waste Less**
When you waste food, you waste the energy used to produce it.

# QUIZ

How much have you learned about climate change? It's time to test your knowledge!

**1. What is the name for the blanket of gases surrounding the Earth?**
a. climate
b. weather
c. atmosphere

**2. What is the main greenhouse gas that cows burp out?**
a. methane
b. carbon dioxide
c. water vapor

**3. Which of these is not a fossil fuel?**
a. coal
b. wood
c. natural gas

**4. How has the gang-gang cockatoo changed to adapt to climate change?**
a. grown a bigger beak
b. moved to a cooler area
c. started eating different foods

The answers are on page 24.

# GLOSSARY

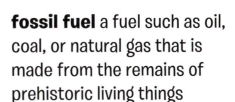

**atmosphere** the blanket of gases that surrounds the Earth

**carbon dioxide ($CO_2$)** a gas that humans and animals breathe out, which is also produced when fossil fuels are burned

**climate** the average weather in a particular place over a long period of time

**electricity** a form of energy that flows as a current, which we can use to power devices

**energy** the ability to do work

**evaporates** turns from a liquid into a gas

**fossil fuel** a fuel such as oil, coal, or natural gas that is made from the remains of prehistoric living things

**fuel** a substance that can be burned to release the energy stored inside it

**greenhouse effect** the warming effect of carbon dioxide and other gases trapping the Sun's heat

**habitat** the place where a plant or animal lives

**heat wave** a long period of unusually hot weather

**satellite** a machine that goes around Earth

# FIND OUT MORE

**Books**

*Climate Change. DKfindout!,* Dorling Kindersley, 2020.

*Our World Out of Balance.* Andrea Minoglio, Blue Dot Kids Press, 2021.

*The Story of Climate Change.* Catherine Barr and Steve Williams, Frances Lincoln Children's Books, 2021.

**Websites**

amnh.org/explore/ology/climate-change

climatekids.nasa.gov

eia.gov/kids/using-and-saving-energy/greenhouse-gases.php

# INDEX

**A C**
animals 8, 9, 16, 17, 21
atmosphere 5, 6, 7, 9, 19
carbon dioxide ($CO_2$) 6, 10, 11, 18, 19, 20

**E F G**
electricity 10, 19
energy 7, 10, 19, 20, 21
floods 12, 15
fuels 6, 9, 10, 11, 19
greenhouse effect 6, 7, 12
greenhouses gases 7, 8, 9, 21

**H I**
heat waves 4, 14
ice 5, 12, 13, 17

**M O**
methane 8, 9, 19
oceans 7, 8, 12, 15

**R S W**
rain 5, 14, 15
storms 4, 5
Sun 6, 7, 15, 18
weather 4, 5, 14
wind 4, 19, 20

Answers: 1. c; 2. a; 3. b; 4. a